Leisure Arts 42

Mastering Watercolour

Tom McArthur

SEARCH PRESS

Introduction

Today, the beauty of watercolour is being appreciated more than ever, as large numbers of painters strive to master the art. It is probably the most testing medium in which to work, yet approaching it thoughtfully can reduce or eliminate the distress that failure brings. A loose style of working can reveal watercolour at its best, due to the atmospheric quality for which the medium is noted, and approaching it in this way will help you to discover both its breadth and limitations. With this understanding you can then move on, with confidence, to handle a more detailed style of work.

When I began to develop my own technique I spent some time working in monochrome, in order to master tonal values, the flow of the paint, and its general handling. It was worthwhile. Whatever your ability, to be a good watercolourist you really require a self-discipline, which, with training, will eventually develop into a natural ability to handle the medium with confidence. Try not to overwork the paint, but endeavour to decide the way in which it is to be applied to the paper before you begin. By doing this you will preserve its freshness, and a clean beauty will be your reward.

Your approach to the subject being painted is of great importance, as it is a matter of deciding what to do with the subject rather than just trying to copy it as it appears. Simplifying it will help to supply the depth, or third dimension, which has to be created. In other words, painting is something of an illusion – hence the need for skill. A point to consider also is the effect upon those viewing your pictures. By simplifying your subject you will allow the viewer some scope for imagination. Such work will have character and attract in a personal way. You have only to look at Turner and the Impressionists to see this working.

Painting is a form of personal expression. So, when learning from others it is really a matter of benefiting from their experience, both in the management of the medium and in the principles of good art in general. You are then free to use this knowledge in a personal way.

The demonstration paintings which follow have been designed not only to help you to grasp the essentials of good watercolour painting but also, hopefully, to enthuse and inspire you.

Materials

The range of materials that you will require is not extensive, and it is worth buying the best quality items that you can afford.

Paints

Watercolour paints can be obtained in tubes, and these enable you to obtain a good mix of colours, especially for large areas. Spending time mixing your own colours is the best way to get to know them first-hand and is more valuable than any advice that can be given.

In general, I recommend that you select only a few colours per picture, say four at the most. This will help you to avoid the visual jumpiness caused by the overuse of colour. A good range from which to choose is lemon yellow, cadmium yellow, yellow ochre (used sparingly), raw sienna, vermilion red, cadmium red, light red, burnt sienna, cobalt blue, ultramarine blue, monestial or Winsor blue, viridian, and ivory black.

Viridian and ivory black should be used only to modify other colours. However, they will extend your range and provide the unusual. Limit the use of opaque colours, such as cerulean blue and chrome yellow, which have a thick texture. Also, avoid ready-made greens, purples, mauves, and greys, which, although tempting, are not essential and are less harmonious than those which you can mix yourself.

Brushes

Sable brushes are the best, although they are very expensive, and it is possible to buy part-sable brushes which are cheaper. Nos. 6, 8, 12, and 14 are useful sizes. Also, I find a 2cm (¾in) flat filbert-shaped mixture and a No. 2 long-haired nylon 'rigger' valuable. Generally, nylon brushes are less suitable, since they do not hold water so well as mixtures and they tend to be somewhat stiffer. However, it is often the artist's handling technique which is at fault, rather than the brush.

After painting, remember to wash your brushes in soap and water, making sure that you get down to the ferrule. Rinse them well, then shape them and either stand them up to dry or lay them in a tray with the hairs clear of the edge.

Papers

Papers over 300gsm (140lb) in weight will not need stretching, and an acid-free 'Not' surface paper is suitable for most subjects. Experiment with different papers to find one that suits you, or seek advice from a good art shop.

I never soak my paper or apply water to it before painting, as I prefer to have full control. Wetting the paper first destroys the sized surface, which is there to prevent premature absorption.

When working, secure your paper to a stout board with clips. Remember to release them at each stage of the painting when the paper is moist, in order to allow it to settle when drying.

Technique

Planning your work first, before starting to paint, will contribute greatly towards your success in using the watercolour medium. Much depends upon the style of work that you desire. For example, a person requiring detail would naturally give emphasis to drawing, whilst another desiring less definition would greatly relax the structural form. However, all artists should do some drawing studies, apart from painting, in order to acquire a basic understanding of line and proportion.

Personally, I never draw on the painting surface, since I prefer to convey structural form by means of tonal shapes made with the brush. My drawing is confined to a small working sketch which contains the tonal masses and such detail as will appear in the finished work. This I scale up with the brush alone. This provides a relaxed style and preserves the freshness of the medium.

Working sketch

Everything should be decided in the working sketch; composition, tonal arrangement, light source, balance of masses, centre of interest and any supporting features. With watercolour you need to be free to control the medium, so avoid having to solve problems whilst painting – solve them beforehand.

I use a solid graphite pencil for working sketches, as it allows the creation of areas of tone using the side of the

Working sketches

Whitehall, see pages 6–7

The lone tree, see pages 10–11

Riding the swell, see pages 14–15

Hints and tips

Whilst devising your composition, by means of a working sketch, decide whether the picture is to be, for example, generally cool or warm, dynamic, peaceful, atmospheric, or depicting movement. You can then select the colours which will provide the effect intended. Next, decide what to lay in first which will help to unite the whole, what is to be done next, and what may be left until last. If you find some drawing on the paper necessary, then try to keep this to a minimum, as outlining the shapes with a pencil first can result in a tightness which causes a loss of movement and atmosphere.

When painting, remember that the fewer the strokes of the brush, the fresher the paint. Use a china palette or plate and mix the moist colour as it comes from the tube. Then, add water to it gradually to get the depth of tone required, testing the colour frequently on a scrap of paper. Also, have a mount handy to lay over your work at each stage of the painting. This will help to show you the progress that you have made and what you need to do next.

pencil. When sharpened properly, a broad area of tone can be made with one stroke.

The sketches shown here illustrate my planning for some of the pictures in the book. Notice how the areas of tone are created, the balance of the masses, the simplicity of statement, and the light and darker accents which all contribute to an overall unity. It is the change of tonal values together with the accents which give life to each picture.

If things do not go as planned, then do not force the painting to conform to your original intent but do the best with what you have. Rearrange your thinking and preserve the quality of the medium by not overworking the paint.

Stage 1

Whitehall: demonstration

Original size: 203 × 330mm (8 × 13in)
Paper: Not surface, 300gsm (140lb)
Brushes: Nos. 8 and 12 part sable, 2cm (¾in) flat filbert, No. 2 rigger
Working sketch: See page 5

In this painting, my intention was to portray a London scene on a calm, sunny afternoon. I selected just three colours, testing them first by mixing to make sure of the tonal values and the warm and cool areas needed. To preserve a clean transparent effect, I worked very broadly and simply until the final stage, doing no drawing on the painting surface but using the brush alone. Working loosely in this way I was able to minimize overloading and provide a unity throughout the picture. The overlaying of detail was left until the final stage in order to create a proper balance of weights and cool and warm areas. This method helps greatly to produce directness, and ensures good control over the work.

Stage 1

A graduated wash is applied to the dry paper, using a simple palette of cadmium yellow, light red, and cobalt blue. At the top, a touch of light red is added to the cobalt blue to refine it. This is followed by a graduated cadmium yellow and light red mix, and ends with a warm

Stage 2

grey made from cobalt blue and light red. A white strip is left unpainted where the horizon will be.

Stage 2

Scaling up by areas of tone, the main shapes are blocked in using the three colours, keeping the whole as a simple background consisting of varied colour devoid of detail. This retains the freshness of the work and is direct and unlaboured. The darker accents are introduced just before the colour is dry. Edges are softened towards the light which comes from the right in this painting. Notice the small patches of light which have been left.

Stage 3

Stage 3

The trees and main lamppost are added, again keeping to the three chosen colours. Further shadows are applied using a mixture of cobalt blue and light red, except for the one under the tree in the foreground which is given a greenish tinge made from yellow, blue, and a touch of light red. This tinge is repeated also on the right of the foreground.

Stage 4 – the finished painting

The figures and other features are now added, together with a strengthening of colour where necessary. Limited detail is added to the buildings. Finally, touches of vermilion red are introduced on the bus and the figure, adding a little sparkle to the picture.

Stage 4 – the finished painting

Testing colours

As I have mentioned, mixing colours is the best way to get to know their characteristics. This can be made more pleasurable by making shapes and areas of tone in the form of very small pictures, which have little or no detail. This will also train you in the ability to recall the basic elements of a scene and provide valuable practice in composition and simplicity of statement. A box of colours or some pans are quite suitable for these small colour-testing miniatures.

The little picture below (actual size) recalls a visit to the Thames at Marlow. The elements of the scene are brought to mind simply yet effectively – the high trees and church with a spire on the left, the distant bridge and trees on the right. The colours used are raw sienna, cobalt blue, and light red.

It is understandable that most people want to paint quite large works before they are ready. However, too

many failures can be very discouraging and greater progress will be made when less ambitious works are attempted. It is very useful to practise taking in the main features of a scene by concentrating on the masses it contains, noting their shape and tonal weight. There is no need to bother about colour or minor detail at this stage. Later, try to recall the scene in this form using no more than three colours. Your ability to simplify will grow as a result.

The little scene above (actual size) was created purely from my imagination, taking into account, of course, that if I had never seen anything like it then I could hardly have invented it. The colours tested here are raw sienna, cadmium red, and French ultramarine blue. Note the clean simplicity of the mauve-grey mass suggesting trees and how the accents below give it meaning and a certain distance. Using the same three colours, you could paint the same scene several times and obtain a different effect in each one. It all depends upon the mixes of colours that you make.

The lone tree, near Hambridge, Somerset

Original size: 254 × 356mm (10 × 14in)
Paper: Not surface, 300gsm (140lb)
Brushes: Nos. 8 and 12 part sable, No. 2 rigger
Working sketch: See page 5

I came across this rather weather-beaten tree, standing alone, when picking my way to the river Isle for an afternoon's fishing. I stopped to make a sketch of the scene on a small pad, which I always carry with me wherever I go. Later, when painting the picture, my intention was to catch a simple glimpse of Nature in her battle to survive the elements of temperature and wind which she endures in the open countryside. In order to achieve this effect, I used a relaxed technique consisting of direct strokes with a No. 12 part-sable brush.

As you can see, the detail in the painting has been kept to a minimum, whilst much attention has been given to the tonal areas and their shape. Notice the foreground, for example, where the top edge of the straw-coloured growth rises and falls to give a varied shape to the general mass. An exciting light patch comes below the bush, adding sparkle to the picture and helping to convey distance by its contrast to the soft tones on the horizon.

First of all, a working sketch is made and the planning of the painting is carried out. The colours chosen are lemon yellow, cadmium red, and intense blue, with ivory black used as a modifier.

The sky is a warm grey made from a little cadmium red with a touch of black to cool it, together with a little lemon yellow to soften the mixture. This is washed down to the horizon, lifting off for the lighter parts and watching the edges of the shapes formed. The edges are softened here and there, leaving some crisp to give an atmospheric effect. Then, a very pale wash of lemon yellow, mixed with a touch of black, is laid in from the horizon down to the bottom of the picture. The paper is laid flat to dry.

Next, the tree is positioned and its general shape is painted in using the side of a No. 12 brush. The darker parts and detail are left until later, and the base of the trunk is left unpainted. The base is partly covered by the dried grass which is now painted, together with the fence. The foreground is carefully shaped with upward strokes, using a No. 8 brush, on top of the original yellow wash.

Lemon yellow and black make a suitable green and this is varied by adding a little of the blue or red, providing changes of colour and tone with which to work. Various tones of the mix, from very pale to darker shapes, are used to paint in the horizon, the field below, and the middle distance. The bush has been left until now so that its tonal value can be gauged correctly. The last stage consists of adding deeper tones on the tree and applying the smaller details which give full meaning to the scene.

It is surprising how many different colours can be made from the three chosen, together with the black. Notice how at every stage the picture is worked on all over, with no one feature being completed on its own at any stage. This is the way to achieve unity.

When first approached, this kind of subject seems to be very simple, and the tendency is to set about it without any planning with the feeling that it can be managed. However, there is more to it than at first appears. For example, if the tree is given priority, then the result will be that its true relationship with the remainder of the scene is lost. The foreground can also present a problem, and, despite its simplicity, needs to be handled carefully. The danger here is the possibility of overworking the paint to the extent that freshness is not achieved.

Always plan beforehand what you intend to portray, then work out the stages which will provide the effect that you desire. Directness of statement, which keeps the paint fresh, is only achieved in this way.

Ice-bound Thames

Original size: 280 × 356mm (11 × 14in)
Paper: Not surface, 425gsm (200lb)
Brushes: 2cm (¾in) flat filbert mixture, No. 2 rigger

A severe winter, a good many years ago, provided the inspiration for this painting.

The main task here is to convey the difference between snow and ice. The snow has a more undulant form, whilst the ice is smooth and flat. The sky is darker than the land in such conditions, and is generally warmer in tone. The bareness of the land in the foreground and middle distance tends to create a silhouette effect with the tree masses.

For this particular picture, the working sketch is slightly larger than usual. The foreground and the middle distance need careful attention due to their rather barren appearance, and the small tonal shapes have to be worked out in terms of size, tonal value, and placing. Also, the treatment of ice and snow has to be decided. Once these decisions have been made the painting operation becomes much easier, and it is possible to concentrate on achieving quality and luminosity in the work.

French ultramarine blue and light red are the only colours which form the palette. The sky consists of a graduated wash using the two colours, ending with a very pale light red at the horizon. The paper used has a slight grain to it, which gives a certain granulation to the masses. The slender trees in the background are 'pulled up' from the main masses, using the rigger. The side of

Working sketch

this brush is used to suggest clumps of foliage. Below the horizon, using the white of the paper for the highest lights, the small broken-edged shapes are put in. Varied cool and warm greys can be made from the two colours and care must be taken with their delicate tonal values. The work is then laid flat to dry.

A mount is now placed over the work in order to judge the positioning of the ice-bound barge. This feature is carefully painted with a warm mixture of the two colours, using the white of the paper to contribute to its form. Notice how the barge blends nicely with the tree masses above it. The frozen river on the left of the picture now receives the delicate reflection of the bushes above, using a delicate warm grey. Any minor additions, in the form of accents, are made now to ensure unity and balance.

The main, darker masses are of great importance in such a picture, demanding care with their shape and tonal value. Notice also how the colour changes from warm to cool and back to warm again, providing both interest and variety. This is a simple picture in content, yet it requires considerable thought and care.

Riding the swell: demonstration

Original size: 241 × 330mm (9½ × 13in)
Paper: Not surface, 300gsm (140lb)
Brushes: 2cm (¾in) flat filbert, No. 8 part sable, No. 2 rigger
Working sketch: See page 5

This is a formidable subject and care must be taken not to overwork it. Again, it is a matter of planning well before starting to paint. For the sake of directness, the number of stages should be kept to a minimum. Although the boat is in the middle of the picture, the land to the left helps to disguise the fact, and balance is achieved by the distant shipping on the right.

The sea is an ever-moving subject with changing shapes and, therefore, difficult to draw when watching it. The thing to do is to just watch it for some time, until an overall general pattern of movement becomes apparent. You will then be better able to simplify its character. Unless the sea is very calm, some sort of direction should be deliberately created in your picture. At the same time, do not forget to study the sky and its relationship with the motion of the sea.

Stage 1

Three colours, yellow ochre, light red, and intense blue, are used. The sky consists of blended washes, wet in wet, using pale mixtures of the red and the blue. The paper is covered down to the horizon in this way, lifting off for the lighter parts. The remainder of the paper, under the sea, is moistened with an extremely pale wash of blue, which slightly tones down the white of the paper. The general shapes and direction of movement in the sky are indicated as moving from left to right. The strongest light is left above the position of the land. Careful attention is paid to the edges of the shapes made.

Stage 2

The shapes and tones in the sea are planned in the working sketch (see page 5), and the changes of colour to be used are first tested on a separate piece of paper. This enables the sea to be painted as simply as possible, following the broad shapes previously designed and using the colours tested. The greens of the sea are made

Stage 1

Stage 2

Stage 3 – the finished painting

from intense blue and yellow ochre. A little light red is added to the blue and yellow for darker shapes. An unpainted gap is left on the horizon at the point where the boat is to be painted in. The tone of the land can now be judged correctly and painted in. Notice how small portions of the original ground are left unpainted in the sea to form the lightest shapes.

Stage 3 – the finished painting

The boat is now painted, taking care to relax the detail in order to convey movement. Parts of the hull are lifted off and softened, and then allowed to dry, after which touches of bluish green are added to give an impression of spray. A little yellowish tinge is introduced into the sea below the boat. The sails of the distant shipping, a very pale light red, are carefully placed to complete the picture.

Loosening up: demonstration

Original size: 82 × 177mm (3¼ × 7in)
Paper: Not surface, 300gsm (140lb)
Brushes: Nos. 8 and 14 part sable

The excitement of painting lies in the ability to portray, both skilfully and beautifully, some facet of life which stirs the imagination. The key to success is a proper understanding of the medium being used, and I believe that an understanding of the watercolour medium can be best achieved through plenty of practice in handling the water and paint mix.

The following method has been designed to help you to 'loosen up', and the aim is to avoid tightness and to practise getting the paint flowing from the start. First of all, try a small picture of the size illustrated, and ignore the subject-matter to begin with.

Stage 1
This is painted using cadmium yellow, vermilion, cobalt blue, and burnt umber. A varied pattern of shapes is made with delicate pastel shades, covering the whole area. These are blended, wet in wet, leaving a few small white areas. The tone is varied and some of the edges are softened.

Stage 2
Next, a working sketch is made of the content to be superimposed upon the first stage. The content is kept simple, making use of the white areas for the light, and tracing paper is used to see how it fits over the first stage.

The illustration shown here is pure invention, with figures added to give atmosphere and scale. If you are able to invent a scene, then this is an advantage, but for those who find it difficult ideas can be drawn from photographs or suchlike. When you use a photograph to

Stage 1

Stage 2 – the working sketch

obtain content, make a working sketch from it and work from this. Make sure that the dimensions of the sketch are in proportion to the finished painting.

Stage 3 – the finished painting

The content is now painted over the first stage, using the same four colours with a No. 8 part-sable brush. A balance of tonal values, and warm and cool areas, is maintained, blending in where necessary.

Experimenting with colour and shapes in this way increases your knowledge of the medium, and such paintings can be highly original. Always remember to use a light touch with the brush and keep your colour fresh and clean. Never overload the painting with too many features and try to avoid losing quality by overworking the paint; be as direct in your statements as possible.

An alternative painting, worked in a style similar to that of Turner's, is shown overleaf.

Stage 3 – the finished painting

An alternative – in the style of Turner

An alternative in the style of Turner

The content of this painting is very simple. Good use has been made of the light, and the colours in the sky are dramatic and unusual.

It is said that throughout his life, J. M. W. Turner used watercolour interchangeably with oils. Without doubt, his mastery in the watercolour medium is technically responsible for his innovations in oils, above all for their high tonality and for his way of applying pigments. Conversely, his practice in oils caused him to employ the use of hatching and stippling in his later watercolours. Whether one approves or disapproves of Turner's later methods, for, no doubt, he was skilled at producing a pure watercolour, it is possible to see the vast potential of the medium through the legacy that he has left us.

Exploring the characteristics of colours, the production of suitable mixes for various purposes, and the scope of each type of brush and paper will help you to realize some of this potential in your own work.

The Bank of England

Original size: 280 × 330mm (11 × 13in)
Paper: Not surface, 300gsm (140lb)
Brushes: Nos. 8 and 12 part sable, No. 2 rigger

Watercolour is extremely versatile. Quite naturally, it is usually thought of as a delicate medium, but it is capable of producing a strong, powerful effect if that is preferred. Some artists, by nature, tend to like the positivity of a strong picture, whilst others love the simple transparent nature of the medium. As your ability progresses, you will discover your own preferences and develop a style that is yours alone. Personally, I like to produce both the strong and the delicate, and I have included an example of a strong painting opposite.

The content is taken from a black and white photograph, from which a working sketch is made. The tonal areas are established to give form, rather than the production of a line drawing. It is then scaled up in the painting using the brush alone. A unity and harmony throughout the whole picture is obtained by the extensive use of just two well-chosen colours, light red and ultramarine blue.

Firstly, a very pale wash of well-diluted light red is laid over the whole paper and allowed to dry. Next, the general structure of the building is established by areas of cool and warm varied tones, blocking in the main shapes. The lighter areas are left to reveal parts of the original wash. Greater detail is then applied to give the buildings full meaning, and the picture is strengthened by adding the darkest parts. Notice how part of the original very pale wash is left to form the shaft of light in front of the building, and also how the statues on the building are simplified by painting their shadows only. The figures are the last features to be painted in.

Prah Sands, near Penzance: demonstration

Original size: 228 × 330mm (9 × 13in)
Paper: Not surface, 300gsm (140lb)
Brushes: 2cm (¾in) flat filbert, No. 8 part sable, No. 2 rigger

This painting is an example of a more delicate treatment of watercolour, illustrating the translucent quality which the medium can give. Despite its simplicity, it is not an easy subject to tackle, as the scattered points of interest make it difficult to achieve balance. Notice how the points of interest are linked up by using delicate touches on the sand together with the shadows cast by the figures.

You may find it tempting to add strokes to such a subject, should some of the shapes be not to your liking. However, take care not to overwork it, as quality will be lost. Much is left until the last stage, for only in this way is unity achieved.

The colours used for this painting are cadmium yellow, yellow ochre, vermilion red, and cobalt blue.

Working sketch

Stage 1

This simply consists of covering the whole of the paper with a pale graduated wash, changing from cool and getting deeper in tone and colour towards the bottom. The four colours are used in this way to provide an underpainting or foundation for the picture. The brush, either the filbert or a No. 14 round part sable, is swept lightly across the paper from left to right, in one direction only. This minimal working of the paint is the only way to achieve quality and beauty.

Stage 2

Two features are now added; the distant land and the sea. The cliffs are put in with a blue-grey, made from cobalt blue with a touch of vermilion red. The lighter parts are lifted off with a clean half-dry brush, just before the paint dries. No other colour is added yet. The shape of the sea is now established with a very pale wash, using cobalt blue. So far, the picture has little content.

Stage 3 – the finished painting

The figures are now carefully painted in, avoiding too much strength in their tonal values. Their placing is important in order to create a rhythm in the picture. Once the figures are established, it is possible to see immediately where further strengthening of tone and colour is required for balance. The darker blue-green tones are now added below the distant cliffs and blended into the sea, using cobalt blue and yellow ochre. Touches of pale yellow ochre are also introduced on the distant land. Strokes of a slightly deeper blue are added to the sea. In sympathy with the direction of the light, the delicate shadows cast by the figures are painted in, together with the remaining detail.

Stage 1

Stage 2

Stage 3 – the finished painting

Painting figures

These, if well painted, can add a human touch and movement to a picture. Generally, it is wise to keep them to a minimum, adding them only discreetly. Of course, a picture depicting a crowd is a different matter, for then they constitute the main interest.

Help with painting figures can be obtained by studying travel brochures. Cut out pictures of figures showing natural movement, and paste them into a scrap-book for reference. Firstly, try a few in one colour in order to get the shape right. When painting them in a picture, paint the head first, the size that you think it will look at the distance it is to be, then paint the body to go with it. Try to avoid stiffness or a clothes-peg effect, which happens when the legs are too thick and stiff. The examples illustrated here have all been painted with a No. 4 polyester brush, and are included to show character and movement.

Remember, that which looks right in a photograph may not work in paint. You have to tailor the subject to suit the picture. Also, figures tend to look better when the depth of tone is played down, the head often being the darkest spot. As a general rule, it is safer to keep to pastel shades, although a dark silhouette effect can be used to advantage in a strongly painted picture, as in the one on page 19.

So, a good formula is to start with the shape of the head. Leave a little gap for the neck, then shape the width of the shoulders and pull the paint downwards feeling the shape of the arms. Next, pull the paint into the waist of the figure, then swell it out slightly before

tapering off down to almost one leg. It is surprising how well this works! However, as with all things, it is practice that makes perfect. A solid graphite pencil is a splendid tool for attempts at figure work, enabling you to doodle at any moment.

The placing of figures in a painting is very important, since they can help the balance or lead the viewer's eye around the picture, as in the beach scene on page 21. Do not forget that the further away the figure, the less defined and paler the tone should be. Also, remember that the use of shadows helps to add weight to your figures, setting them down on the ground beneath. A general mistake is the tendency to make the heads too large in the first place. A slightly undersized head for its body is not such a bad fault.

The practice of drawing and painting figures is a good form of discipline, for unless thought and care is taken when first attempting them, they will not work. Try to see the motion and the general shape in your mind, and, to help develop this asset, start observing people when you are out. Note the differences due to dress and size relative to distance. Look well first, and then close your eyes and see the image in your mind's eye. Consider that which can be left out, or how a feature can be simplified, in order to leave something to the imagination of the viewer. This form of mental painting will add greatly to your store of knowledge.

I always stand when painting, as this gives distance from eye to paper and freedom of arm movement. I decide or judge first, then make a direct stroke. Nothing is touched again whilst it is still wet. If another tone and colour is introduced into what is there, then the latter is either dry or nearly so.

Practice piece

Original size: 114 × 178mm (4½ × 7in)
Paper: Not surface, 300gsm (140lb)
Brushes: No. 8 part sable, No. 2 rigger

The aim of this exercise is to develop your handling ability further, and it involves creating interesting shapes, lifting off to soften the edges, and attending to the balance of weights, colour and unity. It will also help your powers of invention, and, above all, it is fun!

For this painting, cadmium yellow, burnt sienna, and ultramarine blue are used, with touches of veronese green added to give the work a little sparkle. Firstly, however, a clean flat wash of pale cobalt blue is laid over the whole area to provide a toned ground. This is allowed to dry.

Using burnt sienna, with just a touch of ultramarine blue, the strong, brown bushy trees are then positioned with the side of a No. 8 part-sable brush. The shape of these is formed from the top by four simple downward strokes which pull the paint. The tip of the brush is used to form the trunks. The lighter parts, which give variation, are lifted off just before drying. Everything else in the picture is built around this feature, for this composition is pure invention.

At this stage, the tree clumps just painted appear to be rather strong against the sky. This effect is subdued by adding larger but paler tree masses, using a cool blue-grey made from ultramarine and a touch of burnt sienna. Next, a greenish tree mass is added to the left of the picture to help the balance. Finally, it is all tied together with a few direct strokes, varying the colour and tone.

Although it sounds easy, this exercise must be approached with careful thought, pausing to consider each statement regarding its size, colour, weight, and relationship to others. Keep the paint clean and fresh by using simple and direct strokes of the brush.

House among the trees

Original size: 228 × 330mm (9 × 13in)
Paper: Not surface, 300gsm (140lb)
Brushes: 2cm (¾in) flat filbert mixture, Nos. 8 and 12 part sable, No. 2 rigger

This is a painting of simple content. It is created in three stages, using the 2cm (¾in) filbert brush for the sky, the No. 12 part sable for the tree masses, and the No. 2 rigger for the minor dark touches. The No. 8 part-sable brush is used to put in the figures, which are the final addition to the painting. The colours used are lemon yellow, light red, ultramarine blue, and black.

The first stage consists of a simple sky, beginning at the top with a very pale blue. This is then gently carried around using clean water and taken down to the horizon. A pale wash of lemon yellow is taken from the horizon to the bottom of the picture. It is then laid flat to dry.

In the second stage, the tree masses are painted in a light green, made from lemon yellow and ultramarine blue with a touch of black to refine it. Notice that the whole shapes are painted in this one colour mix first. The mid tones and darkest tones are painted on top of these when the first application is dry. During this process, a white space is left for the house on the left of the picture. This can be carefully positioned by using a very pale blue outline for the shape of the house before the tree masses surrounding it are painted. A mount is laid over the work to judge the balance, then the distant hills on the horizon are painted in, taking care to get the correct tone.

In the final stage, touches of very pale light red and blue-grey are applied to the house, together with a minimum of detail. The darkest accents around the picture are made from a strong mixture of the blue and light red. The figures are then carefully placed.

Green patch in the city

Original size: 228 × 330mm (9 × 13in)
Paper: Not surface, 300gsm (140lb)
Brushes: Nos. 4, 8 and 14 part sable, No. 2 rigger

This picture recalls my memories of Leicester Square, London. It is a bright sunny day, and one can rest on the seats provided in a pleasant enclosure away from the busy traffic and general bustle.

The elements forming the all-important atmosphere are suggested at the expense of accuracy. Small light areas of untouched paper, the broken-edged treatment, the contrast of tone with interesting shapes, and an arresting colour pattern all help to create the sense of heat and gentle movement.

As usual, the picture has to be planned out first and decisions made regarding treatment and colour selection in order to achieve the aim. Once this has been done, by means of a working sketch, the application of paint can be made with the minimum of effort, the shapes simply being scaled up and freely painted. The colours used are cadmium yellow, chrome orange, indigo blue, alizarin crimson, and burnt umber.

The broad, yet flowing, shapes of the buildings in the background are indicated first, a relaxed, coloured tonal pattern with a warm and cool balance being the aim. A light yellow-green wash applied to the bottom of the paper completes the first stage, which is then allowed to dry.

Next, the dark foliage on the left, the railings, and the features of interest at the foot of the buildings are painted in loosely. A mount is placed over the work to judge the balance and unity achieved so far. Reference to the working sketch confirms the need for the features in the foreground, and tree on the right, to complete the picture.

Notice how the touches of orange are used to help the eye to travel around the scene and assist in giving the effect of heat. The seated figures in the foreground help to give a sense of distance and scale. The rather bright green on the right receives the light from the left and the shadows confirm the direction from which the light comes.

The farm: demonstration

Original size: 228 × 330mm (9 × 13in)
Paper: Not surface, 300gsm (140lb)
Brushes: 2cm (¾in) flat filbert mixture, No. 8 part sable, No. 2 rigger

Firstly, a small working sketch is made, for the purpose of deciding the tonal values of the various features and how they are to be linked with each other. The foreground is also worked out, both for balance and to create a sense of distance.

Working sketch

As usual, in order to achieve unity, it is a matter of working from light to dark, avoiding finishing any one feature too soon and leaving the detail as a last application. The small masses in the lighter shades are painted first, working along the horizon and taking care with their shapes and proportion.

The colours used for this subject are yellow ochre, light red, and ultramarine blue, with black as a modifier.

Remember that a touch of ivory black with another colour, or added to a mix, will provide more subtle hues, thus avoiding stark colouring and giving better quality. However, colouring can also be modified by the use of 'glazing'. This consists of painting a pale colour over a painted, dry area, in order to lower the tonal value or to warm or cool it. For example, should the green tree mass on the left of this picture be not in sympathy with the rest of the picture, a pale wash of yellow ochre can be added to warm it and bring it into a better relationship with the rest. This process may be regarded as an adjustment, since the fewer the layers of paint upon one another the better the quality.

Stage 1

The sky is painted with a mixture of ultramarine blue and a touch of black in a varied wash, becoming lighter towards the horizon. A half-dry brush is used to lift off the lightest parts, and the edges are softened carefully. When this is dry, the area just above the horizon is warmed with a very pale light red. Notice how low the horizon is; atmosphere and distance would be lost if it were too high. Next, a pale wash of yellow ochre is applied down to the bottom of the picture, and the paper is laid flat to dry.

Stage 2

The features are now painted, initially in simple light tones. When these are dry, a deeper tone is superimposed upon each to give depth and variety of shape, blending the edges with a half-dry brush. A mount is laid over the painting at this stage, revealing the need for the two tones in the foreground, which can now be judged correctly and painted in.

All detail is left until the last stage. The pale blue distant trees can also be added later, in between the main features, to create a link and a sense of depth.

Stage 1

Stage 2

Try painting a tree mass in one colour using the side of a No. 8 brush. Feel the shape of the tree and change the angle of the brush using single downward strokes. Then, with the tip of the brush, pull down the branches and trunk from the main area. It is important to get the mix right on the palette; add water to paint, not paint to water. Always test the strength on a piece of scrap paper before applying it to your picture. Remember, the less work with the brush in watercolour, the better the quality and the freshness.

Stage 3 – the finished painting

Stage 3 – the finished painting

The final task is to pull together all the elements of the picture, to ensure that a good balance of tone and colour has been achieved. This is the most exciting stage, for it is now that the drama is developed, small details and accents being added to give full meaning to the work. However, it is also the stage at which most caution is needed, to avoid overworking and loss of quality.

In this painting, the tonal values are strengthened only where it is felt necessary. Such applications are usually confined to shadows, to darker touches at the foot of trees and buildings, and to small features such as poles, fences, and marks adding character to the land or ground. If included, then figures should also be left until the final stage.

Summary

Time is the enemy of us all, so use every spare moment to plan pictures in your mind. Decide upon the mood of the subject that you have in mind to paint and think out how it might be achieved. When the opportunity arises to paint, try not to rush to get it down but take time to prepare a working sketch, so that the actual process of painting your picture holds few, if any, problems. Choose just a few colours and make trial mixes to ensure that these will supply the effect that you wish to convey. Be as direct as possible; use a light touch when you apply the paint and remember that the fewer the number of strokes of the brush the better the quality will be.

It is a lovely feeling when you have painted a picture which pleases you, especially when it is better than anything that you have done before. I hope that this little book helps you to achieve this feeling, and that you enjoy the experience of painting in the watercolour medium. An ardent desire to do well accompanied by thoughtful application makes for success, but a good 'splash' now and again is fun.

nr Chalfont St Giles
Bucks.

First published in Great Britain 1992
Search Press Limited,
Wellwood, North Farm Road,
Tunbridge Wells, Kent TN2 3DR

Text, drawings and paintings by Tom McArthur

Text, illustrations, arrangement and typography
copyright © 1992 Search Press Limited

ISBN 0 85532 716 2

Publishers' note
There are references to sable hair and other animal hair brushes in this
book. It is the Publishers' custom to recommend synthetic materials as
substitutes for animal products wherever possible. There are now a
large number of brushes available made of artificial fibres and they are
just as satisfactory as those made of natural fibres.

Distributors to the art trade:

UK

Winsor & Newton,
Whitefriars Avenue, Wealdstone,
Harrow, Middlesex HA3 5RH

USA

ColArt Americas Inc.,
11 Constitution Avenue, P.O. Box 1396, Piscataway, NJ 08855–1396

Arthur Schwartz & Co.,
234 Meads Mountain Road, Woodstock, NY 12498

Canada

Anthes Universal Limited,
341 Heart Lake Road South, Brampton, Ontario L6W 3K8

Australia

Max A. Harrell,
P.O. Box 92, Burnley, Victoria 3121

Jasco Pty Limited,
937–941 Victoria Road, West Ryde, N.S.W. 2114

New Zealand

Caldwell Wholesale Limited,
Wellington and Auckland

South Africa

Ashley & Radmore (Pty) Limited,
P.O. Box 2794, Johannesburg 2000

Trade Winds Press (Pty) Limited,
P.O. Box 20194, Durban North 4016

Composition by Genesis Typesetting, Rochester, Kent

Printed in Spain by Elkar S. Coop.